Contents

Joe *by David McCord* 2
Safe Inside *by Jack Ousbey* 3
Sad *by Michelle Magorian* 4
In Hospital *by Gerard Benson* 5
Brown-River Brown-River *by Grace Nichols* 6
Acorn Haiku *by Kit Wright* 7
Nine Lives *by Sandy Brownjohn* 8
Mama *by Lee Bennett Hopkins* 10
Little Sister *by Nikki Grimes* 14
Night Flight *by Shirley Hughes* 15
The Rescue *by Ian Serraillier* 16
Holidays *by John Foster* 21
Oldpark Road *Traditional* 22
Premonition (for Jonathan) *by Jackie Kay* 23
Index of poem features 24

Joe

We feed the birds in winter,
And outside in the snow
We have a tray of many seeds
For many birds of many breeds
And one grey squirrel named Joe.
But Joe comes early,
Joe comes late,
And all the birds
Must stand and wait.
And waiting there for Joe to go
Is pretty cold work in the snow.

David McCord

Safe Inside

The sky is grey,
The wind is blowing.
The rain is coming,
The light is going.
The night is dark,
The worst of the weather.
But here, inside,
We're safe together.

Jack Ousbey

Sad

I'm sad in my tummy
And I don't know why
I don't feel like playing
I only want to cry.

I don't want a story
I don't want my tea
I just want to have a rest
On somebody's knee.

Michelle Magorian

In Hospital

My tongue is mute.
The words are locked
Inside my head.
Beside my bed
A bowl of fruit,
And you who smile
And talk to me
And hold my hand,
I knew you in
Another time.
I know you still
But cannot speak.
My tongue is dead.
The words are shut
Inside my head.

Gerard Benson

Brown-River Brown-River

Brown-River
Brown-River
Why do you run
You must be trying
To catch-up with someone?

O I'm on my way
To catch-up with the sea
But however fast I run
There's always more of me
Always more of me.

Grace Nichols

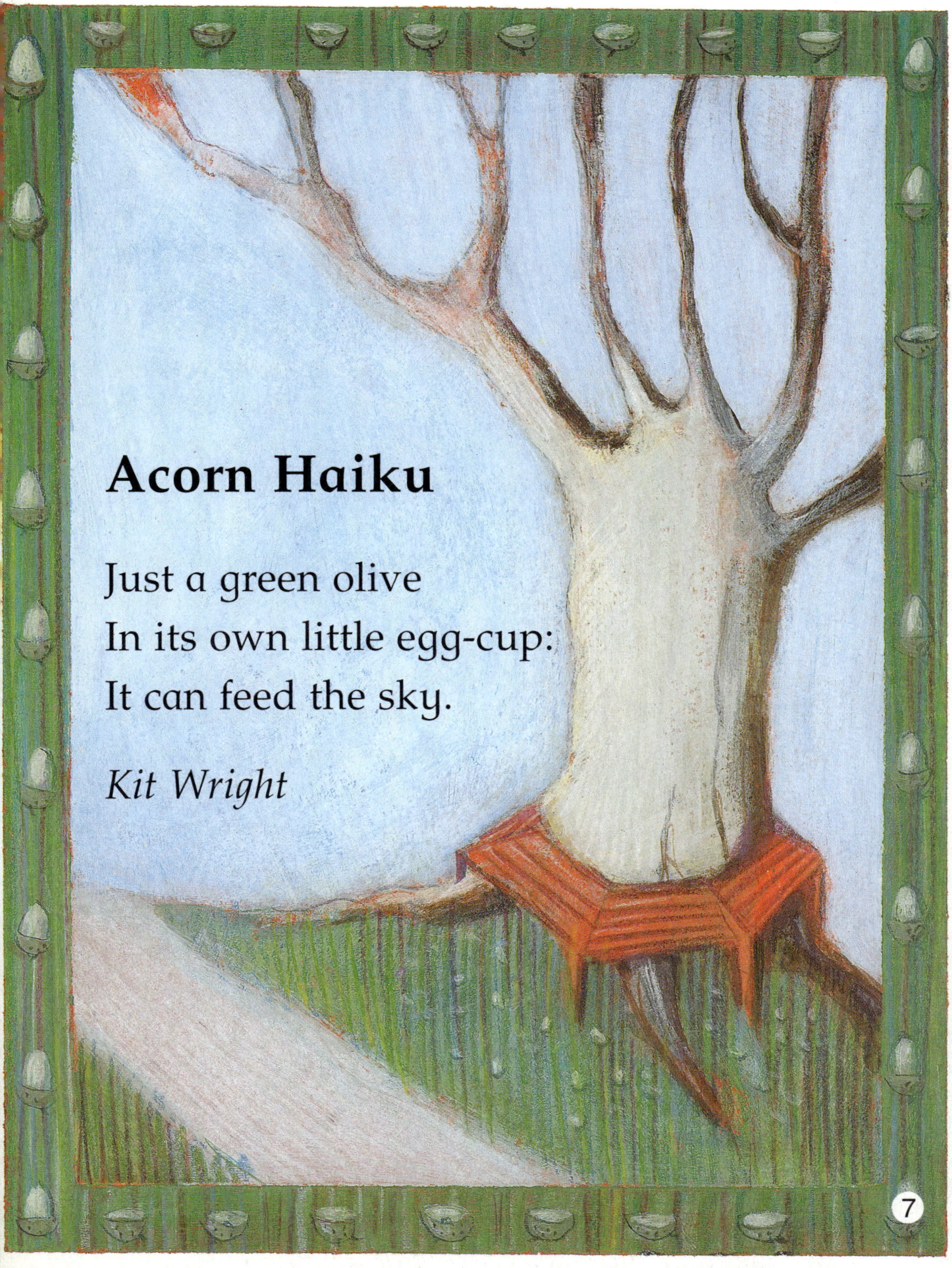

Acorn Haiku

Just a green olive
In its own little egg-cup:
It can feed the sky.

Kit Wright

Nine Lives

i.m. Thisbe (1976-1990)

This is my grave by the holly tree,
Remember me?

I am the cat who arrived by rail
Without a tail.

I am the cat who tried walking on water
Which would not support her.

I am the cat who got stuck on the ledge,
Too near the edge.

I am the cat who was locked in the shed
And could not be fed.

I am the cat who ran in the road
Where traffic flowed.

I am the cat who spat in the night
And lost the fight.

I am the cat who hid out in the snow
When you wanted to go.

I am the cat who with arthritic bones
Concealed her groans.

I am the cat who that Autumn day
Just faded away.

This is my grave by the holly tree.
Remember me.

Sandy Brownjohn

Mama,

looking
tired,
weary,
said,

"Son,
I don't
like that
dreary frown
perched
on your face.

"I know
what's on
your mind.
I know
your *every* look.
I know you
like a book.

“Right now
this dreary place
don’t look like much,
but it will
when I give it
your Mama’s
touch.

“I’ll find
the means
to fix up
this place.

“I’ll put curtains
on these windows.
Saw some
down in
Woolworth’s,
fine ones
starched and stiff
made of
fancy, frilly lace.

"I'll paint
this apartment
head to toe –
the ceilings,
the walls,
the halls.
These rooms'll glow.
This will all be
spanking new
when I get through.
Won't take
no time
for me to do.
No time at all.

"Things'll get better.
I'll make them so.
You'll see.
Have faith in
your Mama.
Believe in me.

“Get some sleep now.
It’s been a rough day.
Think what
tomorrows
will bring our way.”

“‘Night, Mama,”
I said
as I went off to bed,
looking again
at the room’s
empty space
and the
smile-through-a-frown look
on
Mama’s
worn
face.

Lee Bennett Hopkins

Little Sister

little sister
holds on tight.
My hands hurt
from all that squeezing,
but I don't mind.
She thinks no one will
  bother her
when I'm around,
and they won't
if I can help it.
And even when I can't,
I try
'cause she believes
  in me.

Nikki Grimes

Night Flight

Annie flew out of the window,
Bedclothes and cot and all,
And floated around above the ground,
And over the garden wall.

And her shadow skimmed over the gardens
And followed her all the way,
As she looked down on the roofs of the town
And the moon shone as bright as day.

Shirley Hughes

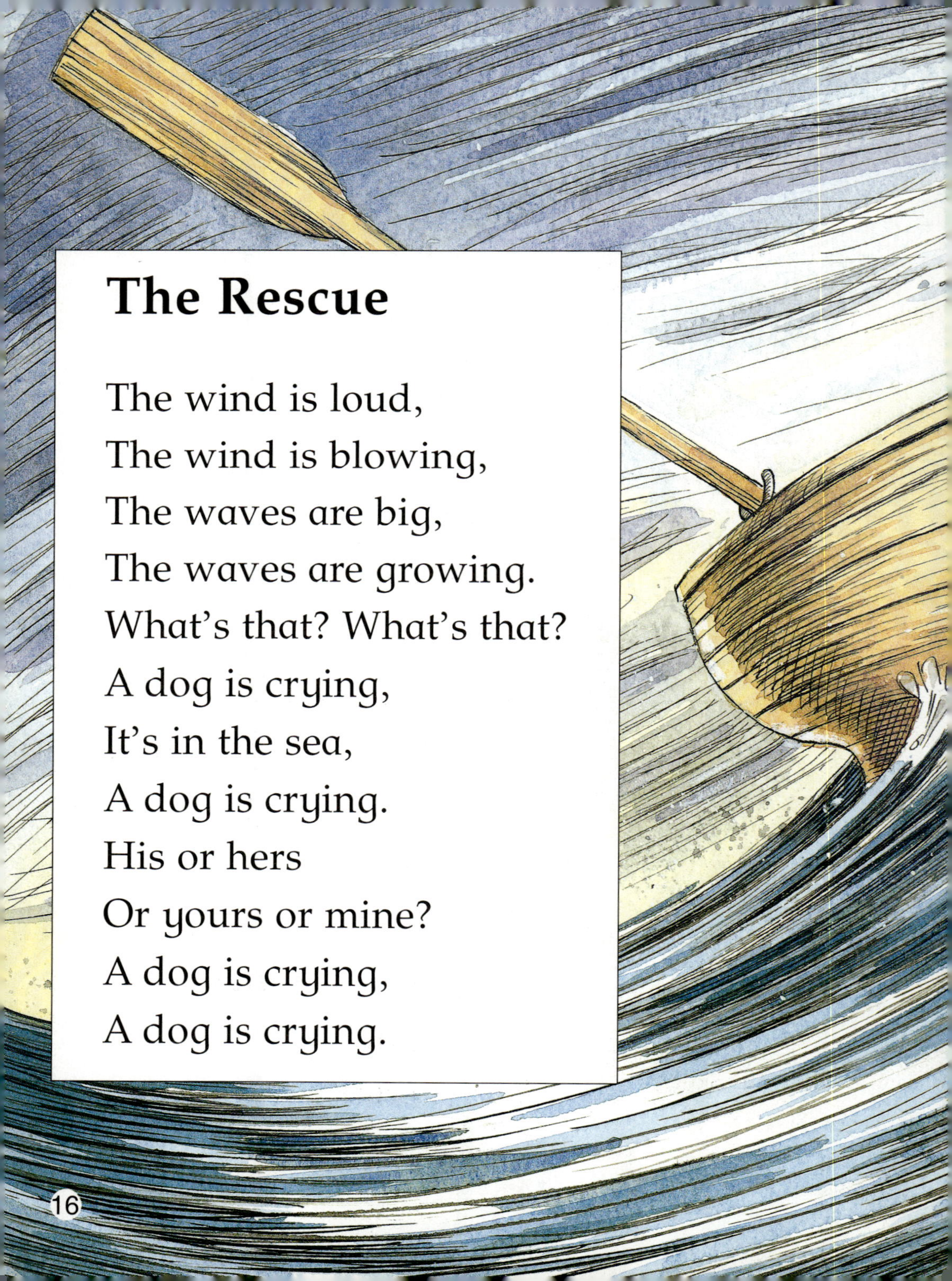

The Rescue

The wind is loud,
The wind is blowing,
The waves are big,
The waves are growing.
What's that? What's that?
A dog is crying,
It's in the sea,
A dog is crying.
His or hers
Or yours or mine?
A dog is crying,
A dog is crying.

Is no one there?
A boat is going,
The waves are big,
A man is rowing,
The waves are big,
The waves are growing.
Where's the dog?
It isn't crying.
His or hers
Or yours or mine?
Is it dying?
Is it dying?

The wind is loud,
The wind is blowing,
The waves are big,
The waves are growing.
Where's the boat?
It's upside down.
And where's the dog,
And must it drown?
His or hers
Or yours or mine?
O, must it drown?
O, must it drown?

Where's the man?
He's on the sand,
So tired and wet
He cannot stand.
And where's the dog?
It's in his hand,
He lays it down
Upon the sand.
His or hers
Or yours or mine?
The dog is mine,
The dog is mine!

So tired and wet
And still it lies.
I stroke its head,
It opens its eyes,
It wags its tail,
So tired and wet.
I call its name,
For it's my pet,
Not his or hers
Or yours, but mine –
And up it gets,
And up it gets!

Ian Serraillier

Holidays

Happy-go-lucky days.
Off out and about days.
Lazy lie-in-bed days.
In front of TV days.
Do as you please days.
Away to the sea days.
You can choose what to do days.
School's over! We're free days!

John Foster

Oldpark Road

On the Oldpark Road, where I did dwell,
Lived a butcher's son, whom I knew
so well,
He courted me, till my heart was sore,
Then left me standing at the door.

He took a strange girl on his knee,
And he told her things that he never
told me,
And now I know the reason why,
Because she had more gold than I.

But her gold will melt,
And his love will die,
And she will be as poor as I.

Traditional

Premonition (for Jonathan)

This kind of thing happens to me all the time:
I dream my hamster has escaped and I wake up
and there it is, buried under a pile of washing.

Or I see my best Aunt in a dream,
where all her lovely thick hair has disappeared,
and the next thing is everyone whispering

in the living room with cups of sweet tea.
Or else my mum climbs a ladder in a nightmare
and falls off it, two weeks later, in real life.

I tell you it spooks me out. It is scary.
Then dreams make things happen, don't they?

Jackie Kay

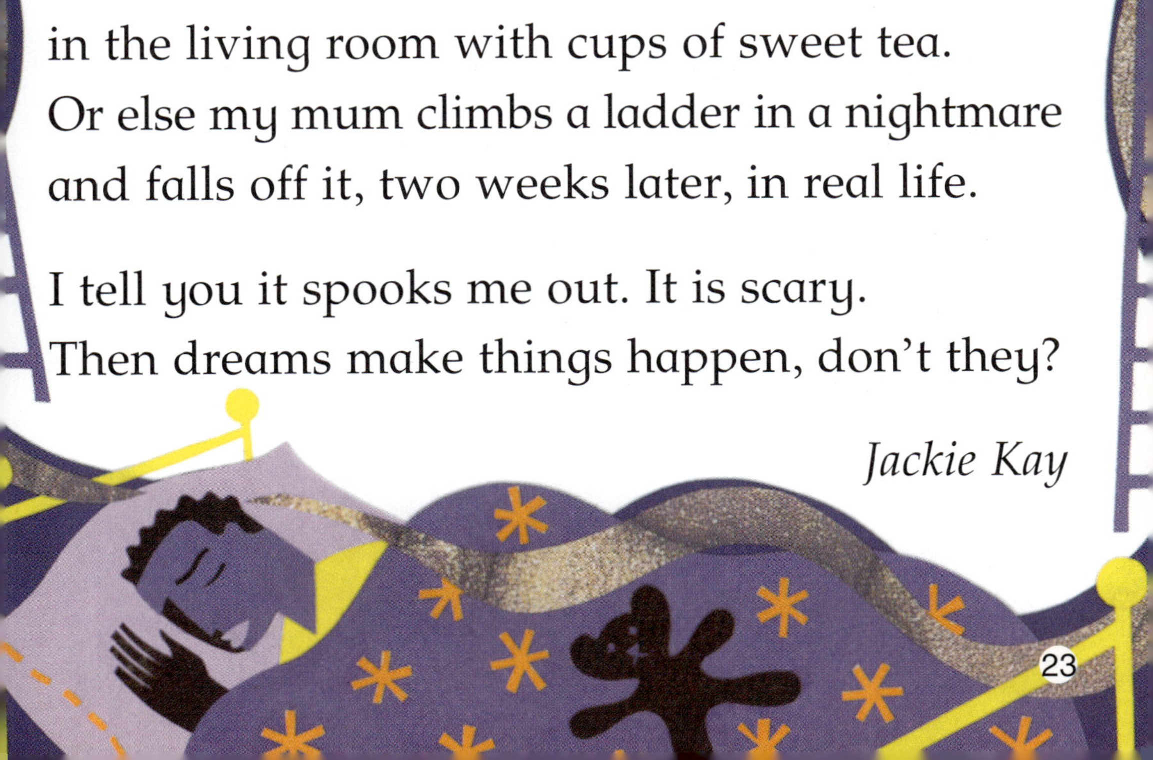

Index of poem features

Ballad 22

Dramatic dialogue 10–13
Dramatic monologue 16–20

Epitaph 8–9

Free verse 5, 14, 23

Haiku 7

Narrative poems 10–13, 15, 16–20

Ode 6

Patterned language 3, 5, 6, 8–9, 10–13, 16–20, 21, 23
Performance poems 10–13, 16–20, 22

Rhyming verse 2, 3, 4, 8–9, 15, 22

Stanzas 4, 6, 15, 22